I0146236

Joseph Addison

Rosamond

An opera. Inscribed to her Grace the Dutchess of Marlborough

Joseph Addison

Rosamond
An opera. Inscribed to her Grace the Dutchess of Marlborough

ISBN/EAN: 9783337309206

Printed in Europe, USA, Canada, Australia, Japan

Cover: Foto ©Thomas Meinert / pixelio.de

More available books at **www.hansebooks.com**

ROSAMOND.

AN

OPERA.

Infcribed to her GRACE the

Dutchefs of MARLBOROUGH.

Hic quos durus amor crudeli tabe peredit
Secreti celant calles, ut myrtea circum
Sylva tegit   Virg. Æn. 6.

By the late Right Honourable

JOSEPH ADDISON, Efq;

LONDON;

Printed for M. Dodsley in Pall-mall, and D.
Cooper in the Strand. M DCC LXV.

TO THE

AUTHOR

OF

ROSAMOND.

————Ne forte pudori
Sit tibi muſa lyræ ſolers, et cantor Apollo.

By Mr TICKELL.

THE Opera firſt Italian maſters taught,
Enrich'd with ſoñgs, but innocent of thought.
Britannia's learned theatre diſdains
Melodious trifles, and enervate ſtrains;
And bluſhes on her injur'd ſtage to ſee
Nonſenſe well-tun'd, and ſweet ſtupidity.

No charms are wanting to thy artful ſong,
Soft as Corelli, but as Virgil ſtrong.

And

From words fo fweet new grace the notes receive,
And mufic Borrows helps, fhe us'd to give..
Thy ftile hath match'd what antient Romans knew,
Thy flowing numbers far excel the new;
Their cadence in fuch eafy found convey'd,
That height of thought may feem fuperfluous aid ;
Yet in fuch charms the noble thoughts abound,
That needlefs feem the fweets of eafy found.

Landfchapes how gay the bow'ry grotto yields,
Which thought creates, and lavifh fancy builds!
What art can trace the vifionary fcenes,
The flow'ry groves; and everlafting greens,
The babling founds that mimic Echo plays,
The fairy fhade, and its eternal maze,
Nature and art in all their charms combin'd,
And all Elyfium to one view confin'd !
No farther could imagination roam,
'Till Vanbrugh fram'd, and Marlbro' rais'd the dome;

Ten thoufand pangs my anxious bofom tear;
When drown'd in tears I fee th' imploring fair :
When bards lefs foft the moving words fupply,
A feeming juftice dooms the nymph to die;
But here fhe begs, nor can fhe beg in vain,
(In dirges thus expiring fwans complain)
Each verfe fo fwells, expreffive of her woes,
And ev'ry tear in lines fo mournful flows;
We, fpite of fame, her fate revers'd believe,
O'erlook her crimes, and think fhe ought to live.

Let joy tranfport fair Rofamonda's fhade,
And wreaths of myrtle crown the lovely maid.
While now perhaps with Dido's ghoft fhe roves,
And hears and tells the ftory of their loves,
Alike they mourn, alike they blefs their fate,
Since love, which made 'em wretched, makes em
    great,
Nor longer that relentlefs doom bemoan,
Which gain'd a Virgil, and an Addifon.

                          Accept,

Accept, great monarch of the Britifh lays,
The tribute fong an humble fubject pays.
So tries the artlefs lark her early flight,
And foars, to hail the god of verfe and light.
Unrival'd as thy merit be thy fame,
And thy own laurels fhade thy envy'd name:
Thy name, the boaft of all the tuneful choir,
Shall tremble on the ftrings of ev'ry lyre;
While the charm'd reader with the thought com-
    plies.
Feels correfponding joys or forrows rife,
And views thy Rofamond with Henry's eyes.

Dramatis

Dramatis Perſonae.

M E N.

King Henry.

Sir Truſty, keeper of the bower.

Page.

Meſſenger.

W O M E N.

Queen Elinor.

Roſamond.

Gridiline, wife to Sir Truſty.

Guardian Angels, &c.

S C E N E Woodſtock-Park.

R O S A M O N D.

ACT I. SCENE. I.

A Profpect of Woodftock-Park, *terminating in the Bower.*

Enter QUEEN *and* PAGE.

QUEEN.

WHAT place is here!
  What fcenes appear !
Where-e'er I turn my eyes;
All around
 Enchanted ground
 And foft Elyfiums rife :
Flow'ry mountains,
Moffy fountains;
 Shady woods,
 Chryftal floods,
  With wild variety furprife.
' *As o'er the hollow vaults we walk,
' A hundred echos round us talk :
 ' From hill to hill the voice is toft,
  ' Rocks rebounding,
  ' Caves refounding,
 ' Not a fingle word is loft.

PAGE.

There gentle Rofamond immured
Lives from the world and you fecured.

 * Alluding to the famous echo in Woodftock-Park.
      QUEEN.

QUEEN.

Curfe on the name ! I faint, I die,
With fecret pangs of jealoufy.———   [*Afide*.

PAGE.

There does the penfive beauty mourn,
And languifh for her Lord's return.

QUEEN.

Death and confufion! I'm too flow———   [*Afide*.
Show me the happy manfion, fhow———

PAGE.

Great Henry there———

QUEEN.

Trifler, no more !———

PAGE.

——— Great Henry there
Will foon forget the toils of war.

QUEEN.

No more ! the happy manfion fhow
That holds this lovely guilty foe.
My wrath, like that of heav'n, fhall rife,
And blaft her in her Paradife.

PAGE.

' Behold on yonder rifing ground
    ' The bower, that wanders
    ' In meanders,
    ' Ever bending,
    ' Never ending,
    ' Glades on glades,
    ' Shades in fhades,
  ' Running an eternal round.

QUEEN.

In fuch an endlefs maze I rove,
Loft in labyrinths of love.
    My breaft with hoarded vengeance burns,

While

While fear and rage
With hope engage,
And rule my wav'ring foul by turns.

PAGE.

The path yon verdant field divides,
Which to the foft confinement guides.

QUEEN.

Eleonora, think betimes,
What are thy hated rival's crimes!
Whether, ah whether doft thou go!
What has fhe done to move thee fo?
—Does fhe not warm with guilty fires.
The faithlefs Lord of my defires?
Have not her fatal arts remov'd
My Henry from my arms?
'Tis her crime to be lov'd,
'Tis her crime to have charms.
Let us fly, let us fly,
She fhall die, fhe fhall die.
' I feel, I feel my heart relent:
' How could the fair be innocent.!
' To a monarch like mine,
' Who would not refign!
' One fo great and fo brave
' All hearts muft enflave.

PAGE.

Hark, hark! what found invades my ear?
The conqueror's approach I hear.
' He comes, victorious Henry comes!
' Hautboys, trumpets, fifes and drums,
' In dreadful concert join'd,
' Send from afar
' A found of war,
' And fill with horror ev'ry wind.

QUEEN.

QUEEN.

Henry returns, from danger free!
Henry returns!——but not to me.
He comes his Rofamond to greet,
And lay his laurels at.her feet,
His vows impatient to renew;
His vows, to Eleonora due.
Here fhall the happy Nymph detain,
(While of his abfence I complain)
Hid in her mazy, wanton bower,
My lord, my life,. my conqueror.
 ' No, no, 'tis decree!
 ' The traitrefs fhall bleed ;.
 ' No fear fhall alarm,
 ' No pity difaim ;
 ' Io my rage fhall be feen·
 ' The revenge of a Queen.

SCENE II.

The Entry of the Bower.

Sir TRUSTY, Knight of the Bower, *folus.*

 ' How unhappy is he,
 ' That is ty'd to a fhe,
  ' And fam'd for his wit and his beauty !
 ' For of us pretty fellows
 ' Our wives are fo jealous,
  ' They ne'er have enough of our duty.
But hah ! my limbs begin to quiver,
I glow, I burn, I freeze, I fhiver ;
  Whence rifes this convulfive ftrife ?
  I fmell a fhrew !
  My fears are true,
  I fee my wife.   SCENE

SCENE III.

GRIDELINE *and* Sir TRUSTY.

GRIDELINE.
Faithless varlet, art thou there?

Sir TRUSTY.
My love, my dove, my charming fair!

GRIDELINE.
Monster, thy wheedling tricks I know.

Sir TRUSTY.
Why wilt thou call thy turtle so!

GRIDELINE.
Cheat not me with false caresses.

Sir TRUSTY.
Let me stop thy mouth with kisses.

GRIDELINE.
Those to fair Rosamond are due.

Sir TRUSTY.
She is not half so fair as you.

GRIDELINE.
She views thee with a lover's eye.

Sir TRUSTY.
I'll still be thine, and let her die.

GRIDELINE.
No, no, 'tis plain. Thy frauds I see,
Traitor to thy King and me!

Sir TRUSTY.
' O Grideline! consult thy glass,
' Behold that sweet bewitching face,
' Those blooming cheeks, that lovely hue!
' Ev'ry feature
' (Charming creature)
' Will convince you I am true.

GRI-

GRIDELINE.

' O how bleſt were Grideline,
' Could I call Sir Truſty mine !
' Did he not cover amorous wiles
' With ſoft, but ah ! deceiving ſmiles :
' How ſhould I revel in delight,
' The ſpouſe of ſuch a peerleſs Knight !

Sir TRUSTY.

At length the ſtorm begins to ceaſe,
I've ſooth'd and flatter'd her to peace.
'Tis now my turn to tyrannize :   [*Aſide*.
I feel, I feel my fury riſe !
Tigreſs, be gone.

GRIDELINE.

——I love thee ſo
        I cannot go.

Sir TRUSTY.

Fly from my paſſion, Beldame, fly !

GRIDELINE.

Why ſo unkind, Sir Truſty, why ?

Sir TRUSTY.

Thou'rt the plague of my life.

GRIDELINE.

I'm a fooliſh, fond wife.

Sir TRUSTY.

Let us part,
Let us part.

GRIDELINE.

Will you break my poor heart ?
Will you break my poor heart ?

Sir TRUSTY.

I will if I can.

GRIDELINE.

O barbarous man !
From whence doth all this paſſion flow ?

ROSAMOND,

Sir **T R U S T Y**.

‘ Thou art ugly and old,
‘ And a villanous fcold.

G R I D E L I N E.

‘ Thou art a ruftick to call me fo.
‘ I'm not ugly, nor old,
‘ Nor a villanous fcold,
‘ But thou art a ruftick to call me fo.
‘ Thou, traitor, adieu !

Sir **T R U S T Y**.

Farewel, thou fhrew !

G R I D E L I N E.

‘ Thou traitor.

Sir **T R U S T Y.**

‘ Thou fhrew !

B O T H.

‘ Adieu ! Adieu !   [*Exit* Grid.

Sir **T R U S T Y** *folus.*

How hard is our fate,
Who ferve in the ftate,
And fhould lay out our cares
On publick affairs ;
-When conjugal toils,
And family broils
Make all our great labours mifcarry !
Yet this is the lot
Of him that has got
Fair Rofamond's bower,
With the clew in his power,
And is courted by all,
Both the great and the fmall,
As principal pimp to the mighty King Harry.
But fee, the penfive fair draws near :
I'll at a diftance ftand and hear.

SCENE

B

SCENE IV.

ROSAMOND *and* Sir TRUSTY.

ROSAMOND.

From walk to walk, from fhade to fhade,
From ftream to purling ftream convey'd,
Through all the mazes of the grove,
Through all the mingling tracks I rove,
　　　Turning,
　　　Burning,
　　　Changing,
　　　Ranging,
Full of grief and full of love,
Impatient for my Lord's return
I figh, I pine, I rave, I mourn.
' Was ever paffion crofs'd like mine ?
　　' To rend my breaft,
　　' And break my reft,
　　' A thoufand thoufand ills combine.
　　' Abfence wounds me,
　　' Fear furrounds me,
　　' Guilt confounds me,
' Was ever paffion crofs'd like mine ?

Sir TRUSTY.

What heart of ftone
Can hear her moan,
And not in dumps fo doleful join !　　　　[*Apart.*

ROSAMOND.

How does my conftant grief deface
The pleafures of this happy place !
In vain the fpring my fenfes greets
In all her colours, all her fweets;
　　To me the rofe
　　No longer glows,
　　Every plant
　　Has loft his fcent:

The vernal blooms of various hue,
The bloffoms frefh with morning dew,
The breeze, that fweeps thefe fragrant bowers,
Fill'd with the breath of op'ning flow'rs,
 Purple fcenes,
 Winding greens,
 Glooms inviting,
 Birds delighting,
(Nature's foftelt, fweeteft ftore)
Charm my tortur'd foul no more.
' Ye powers, I rave, I faint, I die:
' Why fo flow! great Henry, why!
 ' From death and alarms
 ' Fly, fly to my arms,
' Fly to my arms, my monarch, fly !
  Sir T R U S T Y.
How much more blefs'd would lovers be,
Did all the whining fools agree
To live like Grideline and me ! [*Apart.*

  R O S A M O N D.
O Rofamond, behold too late,
And tremble at thy future fate !
Curfe this unhappy, guilty face,
Every charm, and every grace,
That to thy ruin made their way,
And led thine innocence aftray :
At home thou feeft thy Queen enraged,
Abroad thy abfent Lord engaged
In wars, that may our loves disjoin,
And end at once his life and mine.
  Sir T R U S T Y.
Such cold complaints befit a Nun :
If fhe turns honeft, I'm undone ! [*Apart.*
       R O-

ROSAMOND.

' Beneath fome hoary mountain
 ' I'll lay me down and weep,
' Or near fome warbling fountain
 ' Bewail myfelf afleep ;
'. Where feather'd choirs combining
 ' With gentle murm'ring ftreams,
' And winds in confort joining,
 ' Raife fadly-pleafing dreams. [Ex. *Rof.*

   Sir T R U S T Y *folus.*

What favage tiger would not pity
A damfel fo diftrefs'd and pretty !
But hah ! a found my bower invades,

     [*Trumpets flourifh.*

And echo's through the winding fhades ;
'Tis Henry's march ! the tune I know :
A meffenger ! It muft be fo.

SCENE V.

A MESSENGER *and* Sir TRUSTY.

MESSENGER.

Great Henry comes ! with love oppreft ;
Prepare to lodge the royal gueft.
From purple fields with flaughter fpread,
From rivers chok'd with heaps of dead,
From glorious and immortal toils,
Loaden with honour, rich with fpoils,
Great Henry comes ! Prepare thy bower
To lodge the mighty conquerour.

   Sir T R U S T Y.

The bower and Lady both are dreft,
And ready to receive their gueft.

   MESSENGER.

Hither the victor flies, (his Queen
And royal progeny unfeen ;)

Soon as the Britifh fhores he reached,
Hither his foaming courfer ftretched:
And fee! his eager fteps prevent
The meffage that himfelf hath fent!

Sir T R U S T Y.

Here will I ftand.
With hat in hand,
  Obfequioufly to meet him,
And muft endeavour
At behaviour,.
  That's fuitable to greet him.

S C E N E VI.

Enter King HENRY *after a flourifh of Trumpets.*

K I N G.

Where is my love! my Rofamond!

Sir T R U S T Y.

Firft, as in ftricteft duty bound,.
  I kifs your royal hand:

K I N G.

Where is my life! my Rofamond!

Sir T R U S T Y.

Next with fubmiffion moft profound,
  I welcome you to land.

K I N G.

Where is the tender, charming fair!

Sir T R U S T Y.

Let me appear, great Sir, I pray,
Methodical in what I fay.

K I N G.

Where is my love, O tell me where!

Sir T R U S T Y.

For when we have a Prince's ear,
  We fhould have wit;

To

B 3

To know what's fit
For us to fpeak, and him to hear.

KING.

Thefe dull delays I cannot bear.
Where is my love, O tell me where !

Sir TRUSTY.

I fpeak, great Sir, with weeping eyes,
She raves, alas ! fhe faints, fhe dies.

KING.

What doft thou fay ? I fhake with fear.

Sir TRUSTY.

Nay, good my Liege, with patience hear.
She raves, and faints, and dies, 'tis true ;
But raves, and faints, and dies for you.

KING.

' Was ever Nymph like Rofamond,
' So fair, fo faithful, and fo fond,
' Adorn'd with ev'ry charm and grace !
   ' I'm all defire
   ' My heart's on fire,
' And leaps and fprings to her embrace.

Sir TRUSTY.

At the fight of her lover
She'll quickly recover.
      What place will you chufe
      For fift interviews?

KING.

Full in the center of the grove,
In yon pavilion made for love,
Where woodbines, rofes , jeffamines,
Amaranths. and eglantines,
With intermingling fweets have wove
The parti-colour'd gay alcove.

Sir T R U S T Y.

Your Highnefs, Sir, as I prefume,
Has chofe the moft convenient gloom;
There's not a fpot in all the park
Has trees fo-thick, and fhades fo dark.

K I N G.

Mean while with due attention wait
To guard the bower, and watch the gate;
Let neither envy, grief, nor fear,
Nor love fick jealoufy appear;
Nor fenfelefs pomp, nor noife intrude
On this delicious folitude;
But pleafure reign through all the grove,
And all be peace, and all be love.
‘ Oh the pleafing pleafing anguifh
‘ When we love, and when we languifh!
  ‘ Whifhes rifing!
  ‘ Thoughts furprifing!
  ‘ Pleafure courting!
  ‘ Charms tranfporting!
  ‘ Fancy viewing
  ‘ Joys enfuing!
‘ O the pleafing, pleafing anguifh!   [*Exeunt.*

A C T

ACT II. SCENE I.

A Pavilion in the middle of the Bower.

KING and ROSAMOND.

KING.

THUS let my weary foul forget
  Reſtleſs glory, martial ſtrife,
Anxious pleaſures of the great,
  And gilded cares of life.

ROSAMOND.

Thus let me loſe, in riſing joys,
Fierce impatience, fond deſires,
Abſence that flatt'ring hope deſtroys,
And life-conſuming fires.

KING.

Not the loud Britiſh ſhout that warms
The warrior's heart, nor-claſhing arms,
Nor fields with hoſtile banners ſtrow'd,
Nor life on proſtrate Gauls beſtow'd,
Give half the joys that fill my breaſt,
While with my Roſamond I'm bleſt.

ROSAMOND.

My Henry is my foul's delight,
My wiſh by day, my dream by night,
'Tis not in language to impart
The ſecret meltings of my heart,
While I my conqueror ſurvey,
And look my very foul away.

KING.

O may the preſent bliſs endure,
From fortune, time, and death ſecure!

BOTH

BOTH.

' O may the prefent blifs endure !

KING.

My eye cou'd ever gaze, my ear
Thofe gentle founds cou'd ever hear :
But oh ! with noon-day heats oppreft,
My aking temples call for reft !
In yon cool grotto's artful night
Refrefhing flumbers I'll invite,
Then feek again my abfent fair,
With all the love a heart can bear.   [*Exit* King.

R O S A M O N D *fola.*

From whence this fad prefaging fear,
This fudden figh, this falling tear ?
Oft in my filent dreams by night
   With fuch a look I've feen him fly.
   Wafted by angels to the sky.
And loft in endlefs tracks of light ;
While I, abandon'd and forlorn,
To dark and difmal defarts born,
Through lonely wilds have feem'd to ftray,
A long, uncomfortable way.

' They're fantoms all ; I'll think no more :
' My life has endlefs joys in ftore.
' Farewel forrow, farewel fear,
' They're fantoms all ! my Henry's here.

SCENE

S·C E N E II.

A Postern Gate of the Bower.

G R I D E L I N E *and* P A G E·

G R I D E L I N E.

My ſtomach ſwells with ſecret ſpite,
To ſee my ſickle, faithleſs Knight,
With upright geſture, goodly mien,
Face of olive, coat of green,
That charm'd the Ladies long ago,
So little his own worth to know,
On a meer girl his thoughts to place,
With dimpled cheeks, and baby face ;
A child ! a chit ! that was not born,
When I did town and court adorn.

P A G E.

Can any man prefer fifteen
To venerable Grideline !

G R I D E L I N E.

He does, my child ; or tell me why
With weeping eyes ſo oft I ſpy
His whiskers curled, and ſhoe-ſtrings ty'd,
A new Toledo by his ſide;
In ſhoulder-belt ſo trimly plac'd,
With band ſo nicely ſmooth'd and lac'd.

P A G E.

If Roſamond his garb has view'd,
The Knight is falſe, the Nymph ſubdu'd;

G R I D E L I N E.

My anxious boding heart divines
This falſhood by a thouſand ſigns:

Or

Oft o'er the lonely rocks he walks,
And to the foolish Echo talks :
Oft in the glass he rolls his eye,
But turns and frowns if I am by ;
Then my fond easy heart beguiles,
And thinks of Rosamond, and smiles.

P A G E.

Well may you feel these soft alarms,
She has a heart———

G R I D E L I N E.

———And he has charms.

P A G E.

Your fears are too just———

G R I D E L I N E.

———Too plainly I've prov'd.

B O T H.

' He loves and is lov'd.

G R I D E L I N E.

' O merciless fate !

P A G E.

' Deplorable state !

G R I D E L I N E.

' To die———

P A G E.

——— ' To be slain.

G R I D E L I N E.

' By a barbarous swain,

B O T H.

' That laughs at your pain.

G R I D E L I N E.

How shou'd I act ? canst thou advise ?

P A G E.

Open the gate, if you are wise ;
I, in an unsuspected hour,

May

May catch 'em dallying in the bower,
Perhaps their loose amours prevent,
And keep Sir Trusty innocent.

GRIDELINE.

Thou art in truth
A forward youth
Of wit and parts above thy age;
Thou know'st our sex. Thou art a Page.

PAGE.

I'll do what I can
To surprise the false man.

GRIDELINE.

Of such a faithful spy I've need : *
Go in, and if thy plot succeed,
Fair youth, thou may'st depend on this,
I'll pay thy service with a kiss.   [*Exit* Page.

GRIDELINE *sola.*

' Pr'ythee Cupid no more
' Hurl thy darts at threescore,
' To thy girls and thy boys
' Give thy pains and thy joys,
' Let Sir Trusty and me
' From thy frolicks be free.   [Ex. *Grid.*

SCENE III.

PAGE *solus.*

O the soft delicious view,
Ever charming, ever new !
Greens of various shades arise,
Deck'd with flow'rs of various dies;
Paths by meeting paths are crost,
Alleys in winding alleys lost ;

                                        Fountains

* An opening Scene discovers another view of the Bower.

Fountains playing through the trees,
Give coolneſs to the paſſing breeze.
' A thouſand fiery ſcenes appear,
' Here a grove, a grotto here,
' Here a rock, and here a ſtream,
' Sweet deluſion,
' Gay confuſion,
' All a viſion, all a dream !

S C E N E IV.

QUEEN *and* P A G E.

QUEEN.

At length the bow'ry vaults appear !
My boſom heaves, and pants with fear ;
A thouſand checks my heart controul,
A thouſand terrours ſhake my ſoul.

P A G E.

Behold the brazen gate unbarr'd !
—She's fixt in thought, I am not heard —— [*Apart.*

Q U E E N.

I ſee, I ſee my hands embru'd
In purple ſtreams of reeking blood :
I ſee the victim gaſp for breath,
And ſtart in agonies of death :
I ſee my raging dying Lord,
And O, I ſee myſelf abhorr'd !

P A G E.

My eyes o'erflow, my heart is rent
To hear Britannia's Queen lament. [*Aſide.*

Q U E E N.

What ſhall my trembling ſoul purſue ?

C

PAGE.

Behold, great Queen, the place in view!

QUEEN.

Ye pow'rs inftruct me what to do!

PAGE.

That bow'r will fhow
The guilty foe.

QUEEN.

——It is decreed——it fhall be fo;　　　[*After a paufe.*
' I cannot fee my Lord repine
' (O that I could call him mine!)
' Why have not they moft charms to move,
' Whofe bofoms burn with pureft love!

PAGE.

Her heart with rage and fondnefs glows,
O jealoufy! thou hell of woes!　　　[*Afide,*
That confcious fcene of love contains
The fatal caufe of all your pains:
In yonder flowr'y vale fhe lies,
Where thefe fair-bloffom'd arbours rife.

QUEEN.

Let us hafte to deftroy
Her guilt and her joy.
' Wild and frantick is my grief!
' Fury driving,
' Mercy ftriving,
' Heaven in pity fend relief!
' The pangs of love
' Ye pow'rs remove,
Or dart your thunder at my head:
' Love and defpair
' What heart can bear!
Eafe my foul, or ftrike me dead!　　　[*Exeunt.*

SCENE.

SCENE V.

The Scene changes to the pavilion as before.

ROSAMOND *sola.*

' Tranſporting pleaſure ! who can tell it !
' When our longing eyes diſcover
' The kind, the dear, approachiug lover,
' Who can utter, or conceal it !
A ſudden motion ſhakes the grove :
I hear the ſteps of him I love ;
Prepare, my ſoul, to meet thy bliſs !
——Death to my eyes ; what ſight is this !
The Queen, th' offended Queen, I ſee !
——Open, O earth ! and ſwallow me !

SCENE VI.

Enter to her the QUEEN *with a bowl in one
band, and a dagger in the other.*

QUEEN.

Thus arm'd with double death I come :
Behold, vain wretch, behold thy doom !
Thy crimes to their full period tend,
And ſoon by This, or This, ſhall end.

ROSAMOND.

What ſhall I ſay, or how reply
To threats of injur'd majeſty ?

QUEEN.

'Tis guilt that does thy tongue controul,
Or quickly drain the fatal bowl,
Or this right hand performs its part,
And plants a dagger in thy heart.

C 2   ROSA-

ROSAMOND.

Can Britain's Queen give such commands,
Or dip in blood those sacred hands ?
In her shall such revenge be seen ?
Far be that from Britain's Queen !

QUEEN.

How black does my design appear !
Was ever mercy so severe ?   [*Aside.*

ROSAMOND.

' When tides of youthful blood run high,
' And scenes of promis'd joys are nigh,
  ' Health presuming,
  ' Beauty blooming,
' Oh how dreadful 'tis to die !

QUEEN.

To those whom foul dishonours stain,
Life itself should be a pain.

ROSAMOND.

Who could resist great Henry's charms,
·And drive the hero from her arms ?
  ' Think on the soft, the tender fires,
' Melting thoughts and gay desires,
' That in your own warm bosom rise,
' When languishing with lovesick eyes
' That great, that charming man you see :
' Think on yourself, and pity me !

QUEEN.

And dost thou thus thy guilt deplore !
          [*Offering the dagger to her breast.*
Presumptuous woman ! plead no more !

ROSAMOND.

O Queen, your lifted arm restrain !
Behold these tears !

QUEEN.

QUEEN.

——They flow in vain.

ROSAMOND.

Look with compaffion on my fate !
O hear my fighs !——

QUEEN.

——They rife too late.
Hope not a day's, an hour's reprieve.

ROSAMOND.

Tho' I live wretched, let me live.
In fome deep dungeon let me lie,
Cover'd from ev'ry human eye,
Banifh'd the day, debarr'd the light ;
Where fhades of everlafting night
May this unhappy face difarm,
And caft a veil o'er ev'ry charm :
Offended heaven I'll there adore,
Nor fee the Sun, nor Henry more.

QUEEN.

* Moving language, fhining tears,
* Glowing guilt, and graceful fears,
* Kindling pity, kindling rage,
* At once provoke me, and affwage.   [*Afide.*

ROSAMOND.

What fhall I do to pacify
Your kindled vengeance !

QUEEN.

——Thou fhalt die.   [*Offering the dagger.*

ROSAMOND.

Give me but one fhort moment's ftay.
——O Henry, why fo far away ?   [*Afide.*

QUEEN.

Prepare to welter in a flood
Of ftreaming gore.   [*Offering the dagger.*

C 3   ROSA.

30 · *ROSAMOND.*

ROSAMOND.

——O spare my blood,
And let me grasp the deadly bowl.
                    [*Takes the bowl in her hand.*
QUEEN.
Ye pow'rs, how pity rends my soul !   [*Aside.*
ROSAMOND.
This prostrate at your feet I fall.
O let me still for mercy call !   [*Falling on her knees.*
' Accept, great Queen, like injur'd heaven,
' The soul that begs to be forgiven :
' If in the latest gasp of breath,
' If in the dreadful pains of death,
' When the cold damp bedews your brow,
' You hope for mercy, show it now.
QUEEN.
Mercy to lighter crimes is due,
Horrors and death shall thine pursue [*Offering the dagger.*
ROSAMOND.
Thus I prevent the fatal blow,   [*Drinks.*
——Whither, ah ! whither shall I go !
QUEEN.
Where thy past life thou shalt lament,
And wish thou hadst been innocent.
ROSAMOND.
Tyrant ! to aggravate the stroke,
And wound a heart, already broke !
My dying soul with fury burns,
And slighted grief to madness turns.
   ' Think not, thou author of my woe,
   ' That Rosamond will leave thee so :
      ' At dead of night,
      ' A glaring spright,

' With hideous fcreams
' I'll haunt thy dreams ;
' And when the painful night withdraws,
' My Henry fhall revenge my caufe.
O whither does my frenzy drive !
Forgive my rage, your wrongs forgive.
My veins are froze ; my blood grows chill ;
The weary fprings of life ftand ftill ;
The fleep of death benumbs all o'er
My fainting limbs, and I'm no more. [*Falls on the couch.*

Q U E E N.
Hear and obferve your Queen's commands.
[*To her attendants.*
Beneath thofe hills a Convent ftands,
Where the fam'd ftreams of Ifis ftray ;
Thither the breathlefs coarfe convey,
And bid the cloifter'd maids with care
The due folemnities prepare. [*Exeunt with the Body.*
' When vanquifh'd foes beneath us lie,
' How great it is to bid them die !
' But how much greater to forgive,
' And bid a vanquifh'd foe to live !

S C E N E VII.

Sir TRUSTY in a Fright.

A breathlefs corps ! what have I feen !
And follow'd by the jealous Queen !
It muft be fhe ! my fears are true :
The bowl of pois'nous juice I view.
How can the fam'd Sir-Trufty live
To hear his Mafter chide and grieve ?
No ! tho' I hate fuch bitter beer,
Fair Rofamond, I'll pledge thee here. [*Drinks.*
The

The King this doleful news shall read
　　In lines of my inditing :
" Great Sir,   [*Writes.*
　" Your Rosamond is dead
　" As I am at this present writing.
' The bower turns round, my brain's abus'd,
' The labyrinth grows more confus'd,
' The thickets dance——I stretch, I yawn.
' Death has tripp'd up my heels—I'm gone.
　　　　　　　　　　　　[*Staggers and falls.*

S C E N E   VIII.

Q U E E N *sola.*

The conflict of my mind is o'er,
And Rosamond shall charm no more.
　Hence ye secret damps of care,
　Fierce disdain, and cold despair,
　Hence ye fears and doubts remove ;
　　Hence grief and hate !
　　Ye pains that wait
On jealousy, the rage of love.

　　' My Henry shall be mine alone,
　　' The Hero shall be all my own ;
　　' Nobler joys possess my heart
　　' Than crowns and scepters can impart.

　　　　　　　　　　　　　　A C T

ACT III. SCENE I.

SCENE *a Grotto,* HENRY *afleep, a cloud de-fcends, in it. two Angels fuppos'd to be the Guardian Spirits of the* Britifh *Kings in War and in Peace.*

1 ANGEL.

BEHOLD th' unhappy Monarch there,
That claims our tutelary care !

2 ANGEL.

In fields of death around his head
A fhield of adamant I fpread.

1 ANGEL.

In hours of peace, unfeen, unknown,
I hover o'er the Britifh throne.

2 ANGEL.

When hofts of foes with foes engage,
And round th' anointed hero rage,
The cleaving fauchion I mifguide.
And turn the feather'd fhaft afide.

1 ANGEL.

When dark fermenting factions fwell,
And prompt th' ambitious to rebell,
A thoufand terrors I impart,
And damp the furious traitor's heart.

BOTH.

But oh what influence can move
The pangs of grief, and rage of love !

2 ANGEL

I'll fire his foul with mighty themes,
'Till Love before Ambition fly.

1 AN-

1 ANGEL.

I'll footh his cares in pleafing dreams, ·
'Till grief in joyful raptures die.

2 ANGEL.

' Whatever glorious and renown'd
' In Britifh annals can be found ;
' Whatever actions fhall adorn
' Britannia's heroes, yet unborn,
' In dreadful vifions fhall fucceed ;
' On fancy'd fields the Gaul fhall bleed,
' Crefly fhall ftand before his eyes.
' And Agincourt and Blenheim rife.

1 ANGEL.

See, fee, he fmiles amidft his trance,
And fhakes a vifionary lance,
His brain is fill'd with loud alarms ;
Shouting armies, clafhing arms,
The fofter prints of love deface ;
And trumpets found in ev'ry trace.

BOTH.

' Glory drives :
' ' drives !
    ' The field is won !
' Fame revives,
    ' And love is gone.

1 ANGEL.

To calm thy grief, and and lull thy cares,
    Look up and fee
What, after long revolving years,
    Thy bower fhall be !
When time its beauties fhall deface ;
And only with its ruins grace
The future profpect of the place.
    Behold the glorious pile afcending ! †
    Columns fwelling, arches bending,

† Scene changes to the Plan of Blenheim caftle.

Domes in awful pomp arifing,
Art in curious ftrokes furprifing,
Foes in figur'd fights contending,
Behold the glorious pile afcending!

2 A N G E L.

He fees, he fees the great reward
For Anna's mighty Chief prepar'd :
His growing joys no meafure keep,
Too vehement and fierce for fleep.

1 A N G E L.

' Let grief and love at once engage,
' His heart is proof to all their pain ;
' Love may plead————

2 A N G E L.

————' And grief may rage————

B O T H.

' But both fhall plead and rage in vain.

[*The Angels afcend, and the vifion difappears.*

H E N R Y, *ftarting from the Couch.*

Where have my ravifh'd fenfes been ;
What joys, what wonders, have I feen ;
The fcene yet ftands before my eye,
A thoufand glorious deeds that lie
In deep futurity obfcure,
Fights and triumphs immature,
Heroes immers'd in time's dark womb,
Ripening for mighty years to come,
Break forth, and to the day difplay'd,
My foft inglorious hours upbraid.
Tranfported with fo bright a fcheme,
My waking life appears a dream.
' Adieu, ye wanton fhades and bowers,
' Wreath of myrtle, beds of flowers,

' Rofy

' Rofy brakes,
' Silver lakes,
' To love and you
' A long adieu !
O Rofamond, O rifing woe !
Why do my weeping eyes o'erflow ?
O Rofamond ! O fair diftrefs'd !
How fhall my heart, with grief opprefs'd,
Its unrelenting purpofe tell ;
And take the long, the laft farewel !
  ' Rife, glory, rife in all thy charms,
  ' Thy waving creft, and burnifh'd arms,
  ' Spread thy gilded banners round,
  ' Make thy thundering courfer bound,
  ' Bid the drum and trumpet join,
  ' Warm my foul with rage divine;
  ' All thy pomps around thee call :
  ' To conquer love will ask them all.   [*Exit.*

S C E N E II.

*The fcene changes to that part of the bower where
Sir Trufty lies upon the ground, with the bowl and
dagger on the table.*

Enter Q U E E N.

Every ftar, and every pow'r,
Look down on this important hour ;
Lend your protection and defence
Every guard of innocence !
Help me my Henry to affwage,
To gain his love, or bear his rage.

                              ' My-

' 'Mysterious love, uncertain treasure,
' Hast thou more of pain or pleasure !
　　' Chill'd with tears,
　　' Kill'd with fears,
' Endless torments dwell about thee :
' Yet who would live, and live without thee !
But oh the sight my soul alarms ?
　　My Lord appears, I'm all on fire !
Why am I banish'd from his arms ?
　　My heart's too full, I must retire.

　　　　　　[Retires to the end of the stage.

SCENE III.

KING *and* QUEEN.

KING.

Some dreadful birth of fate is near :
Or why, my soul, unus'd to fear,
With secret horror dost thou shake ?
Can dreams such dire impressions make !
What means this solemn, silent show ?
This pomp of death, this scene of woe !
Support me, heav'n ! what's this I read ?
O horror ! Rosamond is dead.
What shall I say, or whether turn ?
With grief, and rage, and love, I burn :
From thought to thought my soul is tost,
And in the whirle of passion lost.
Why did I not in battle fall,
Crush'd by the thunder of the Gaul ?
Why did the spear my bosom miss ?
Ye pow'rs, was I reserv'd for this !

D

' Dif-

' Diſtracted with woe
' I'll ruſh on the foe
   ' To ſeek my relief :
' The ſword or the dart
' Shall pierce my ſad heart,
' And finiſh my grief !

QUEEN.

Fain wou'd my tongue his griefs appeaſe,
And give his tortur'd boſom eaſe.   [*Aſide.*

KING.

But ſee ! the cauſe of all my fears,
The ſource of all my grief appears !
No unexpected gueſt is here ;
   The fatal bowl
   Inform'd my ſoul
Eleonora was too near.

QUEEN.

Why do I here my Lord receive ?

KING.

Is this the welcome that you give ?

QUEEN.

Thus ſhou'd divided lovers meet ?

BOTH.

' And is it thus, ah ! thus we greet !

QUEEN.

What in theſe guilty ſhades cou'd you,
Inglorious conqueror, purſue ?

KING.

Cruel woman, what cou'd you ?

QUEEN.

Degenerate thoughts have fir'd your breaſt,

KING.

The thirſt of blood has yours poſſeſs'd.

SCENE

QUEEN.

' A heart fo unrepenting,

KING.

' A rage fo unrelenting,

BOTH.

' Will for ever .
' Love diffever,
' Will for ever break our reft

KING.

Floods of forrow will I fhed
    To mourn the lovely fhade !
My Rofamond, alas, is dead,
    And where, O where convey'd !
' So bright a bloom, fo foft an air,
    ' Did ever nymph difclofe !
' The lily was not half fo fair,
    ' Nor half fo fweet the rofe.

QUEEN.

How is his heart with anguifh torn !   [*Afide.*
My Lord, I cannot fee you mourn ;
The living you lament : while I,
To be lamented fo, cou'd die,

KING.

The living ! fpeak, oh fpeak again !
Why will you dally with my pain ?

QUEEN.

Were your lov'd Rofamond alive,
Wou'd not my former wrongs revive ?

KING.

Oh no ; by Vifions from above
Prepar'd for grief, and free'd from love,
I came to take my laft adieu.

QUEEN.

How am I blefs'd if this be true ! ———   [*Afide.*

D 2   KING.

KING.

And leave th' unhappy nymph for you.
But O !————

QUEEN.

Forbear, my Lord, to grieve,
And know your Rosamond does live.
' If 'tis joy to wound a lover,
  ' How much more to give him ease ?
' When his passion we discover,
  ' Oh how pleasing 'tis to please !
' The bliss returns, and we receive
' Transports greater than we give.

KING.

O quickly relate
This riddle of fate !
My impatience forgive,
Does Rosamond live?

QUEEN.

The bowl, with drowsy juices fill'd,
From cold Egyptian drugs distill'd,
In borrow'd death has clos'd her eyes ;
But soon the waking nymph shall rise,
And, in a convent plac'd, admire
The cloister'd walls and virgin choire :
With them in songs and hymns divine
The beauteous penitent shall join,
And bid the guilty world adieu.

KING.

How am I blest if this be true !   [*Aside.*

QUEEN.

Atoning for herself and you.

KING.

I ask no more ! secure the fair
In life and bliss : I ask not where :

For

For ever from my fancy fled
May the whole world believe her dead,
That no foul minifter of vice.
Again my finking foul intice
Its broken paſſion to renew,
But let me live and die with you.

Q U E E N.
How does my heart for fuch a prize.
The vain cenforious world defpife,
Tho' diftant ages, yet unborn,
For Rofamond fhall falfly mourn ;
And with the prefent times agree,
To brand my name with cruelty ;
How does my heart for fuch a prize
The vain cenforious world defpife !

But fee your flave, while yet I fpeak,
From his dull trance unfetter'd break !
As he the potion fhall furvive
Believe your Rofamond alive.

K I N G.
O happy day ! O pleafing view !
My Queen forgives———

Q U E E N.
———My Lord is true.

K I N G.
' No more I'll change,

Q U E E N.
' No more I'll grieve:

B O T H.
' But ever thus united live.

Sir T R U S T Y *awaking.*
In which world am I ! all I fee,
Ev'ry thicket, bufh and tree,

So like the place from whence I came,
That one wou'd fwear it were the fame,
My former legs too, by their pace !
And by the whiskers, 'tis my face !
The felf fame habit, garb and mein !
They ne'er wou'd bury me in green;

SCENE IV.

GRIDELINE *and Sir* TRUSTY.

GRIDELINE.

Have I then liv'd to fee this hour,
And took thee in the very bow'r?

Sir TRUSTY.

Widow Trufty, why fo fine ?
Why doft thou thus in colours fhine?
Thou fhould'ft thy husband's death bewail
In fable vefture, peak and veil.

GRIDELINE.

Forbear thefe foolifh freaks, and fee
How our good King and Queen agree,
Why fhou'd not we their fteps purfue,
And do as our fuperiors do ?

Sir TRUSTY.

Am I bewitch'd, or do I dream ?
I know not who, or where I am,
Or what I hear, or what I fee ;
But this I'm fure, howe'er it be,
It fuits a perfon in my ftation
T'obferve the mode, and be in fafhion,
Then let not Grideline the chafte
Offended be for what is paft,
And hence anew my vows I plight
To be a faithful courteous knight.

GRIDELINE.

I'll too my plighted vows renew,
Since 'tis so courtly to be true.

    ' Since conjugal paſſion
    ' Is come into faſhion,
  ' And marriage ſo bleſt on the throne is,
    ' Like a Venus I'll ſhine,
    ' Be fond and be fine,
  ' And Sir Truſty ſhall be my Adonis.

Sir T R U S T Y.

' And Sir Truſty ſhall be thy Adonis.

The K I N G *and* Q U E E N *advancing.*

K I N G.

Who to forbidden joys wou'd rove,
That knows the ſweets of virtuous love ?
Hymen, thou ſource of chaſte delights,
Chearful days, and bliſsful nights,
Thou doſt untainted joys diſpenſe,
And pleaſure join with innocence:
Thy raptures laſt, and are ſincere
From future grief and preſent fear.

B O T H.

' Who to forbidden joys wou'd rove.
' That knows the ſweets of virtuous love ?

F I N I S.

www.ingramcontent.com/pod-product-compliance
Lightning Source LLC
Chambersburg PA
CBHW021443090426
42739CB00009B/1620